MINIBEASTS UP CLOSE

Spiders Up Close

Robin Birch

www.raintreepublishers.co.uk
Visit our website to find out more information about **Raintree** books.

To order:
 Phone 44 (0) 1865 888112
 Send a fax to 44 (0) 1865 314091
💻 Visit the Raintree Bookshop at **www.raintreepublishers.co.uk** to browse our catalogue and order online.

Published in 2004 by Heinemann Library
a division of Harcourt Education Australia,
18–22 Salmon Street, Port Melbourne Victoria 3207 Australia
(a division of Reed International Books Australia Pty Ltd,
ABN 70 001 002 357).
Visit the Heinemann Library website @
www.heinemannlibrary.com.au

First published in Great Britain by Raintree,
Halley Court, Jordan Hill, Oxford OX2 8EJ,
part of Harcourt Education.
Raintree is a registered trademark of Harcourt Education Ltd.

A Reed Elsevier company

© Reed International Books Australia Pty Ltd 2004
First published in paperback in 2005

ISBN 1 74070 188 7 (hardback)
08 07 06 05 04
10 9 8 7 6 5 4 3 2 1

ISBN 1 844 43354 4 (paperback)
09 08 07 06 05
10 9 8 7 6 5 4 3 2 1

Editorial: Carmel Heron, Anne McKenna
Design: Stella Vassiliou, Marta White
Photo research: Legend Images, Wendy Duncan
Illustration: Rob Mancini
Production: Tracey Jarrett

Typeset in Officina Sans 19/23 pt
Pre-press by Digital Imaging Group (DIG)
Printed in China by WKT Company Ltd.

The paper used to print this book comes from sustainable resources.

National Library of Australia Cataloguing-in-Publication data:

Birch, Robin.
    Spiders up close.

    Includes index.
    For primary students.
    ISBN 1 74070 188 7 (hardback)
    ISBN 1 844 43354 4 (paperback)

    1. Spiders - Juvenile literature. I. Title.
    (Series : Birch, Robin. Minibeasts up close).

595.4

Acknowledgements
The publisher would like to thank the following for permission to reproduce photographs: ANT Photo Library/Jim Frazier: p. **14**, /Ken Griffiths: p. **6**, /Otto Rogge: p. **15**, /Cyril Webster: p. **24**; Auscape/Goetgheluck/Pho.n.e.: p. **19**; /Greg Harold: p. **7**, /C. Andrew Henley: p. **10**, /Steven David Miller: p. **5**; Lochman Transparencies/© Stanley Breeden: p. **25** (top), /© Andrew Davoll: p. **22**, /© Jiri Lochman: pp. **11, 25** (bottom), /© Jay Sarson: p. **16**; Nature Focus/Mike Gray: p. **23**; photolibrary.com/Animals Animals: pp. **12, 18**, /Index Stock: p. **29**, /OSF p. **4**, /Photo Researchers pp. **8, 26**, /SPL pp. **17, 19**; © Paul Zborowski pp. **13, 27, 28**.

Cover photograph of a red-back spider reproduced with permission of Lochman Transparencies/© Jiri Lochman.

Every attempt has been made to trace and acknowledge copyright. Where an attempt has been unsuccessful, the publisher would be pleased to hear from the copyright owner so any omission or error can be rectified.

Contents

Any words appearing in bold, **like this**, are explained in the Glossary.

Amazing spiders!

Have you seen a spider lately? Have you seen one on a web in a garden? Have you wondered what spiders do all day? Spiders are amazing when you get to know them, close up.

Spiders are not insects. They do not have feelers or wings.

What are spiders?

Spiders belong to a group of animals called arachnids (a-rak-nids). Arachnids are animals with eight legs. A spider has a thin, hard skin called an **exoskeleton** on the outside of its body, instead of bones inside its body.

There are about 35,000 different kinds, or **species**, of spiders. The largest spiders have bodies about as long as a computer mouse (9.5 centimetres). The smallest spiders are smaller than a poppy seed (1 millimetre).

Some spiders build webs to catch insects to eat.

Bird-eating spiders

The largest spiders are the Goliath bird-eating spiders. They hunt at night for mice, frogs, lizards and small birds.

Where do spiders live?

Spiders live in all parts of the world, except Antarctica. They live in all kinds of **habitats**, including in forests, deserts and mountains.

Most spiders eat insects, so spiders live wherever there are insects. Some spiders live in trees and bushes. Some live in the soil, or under stones, rocks, bark or wood. Other spiders live in houses and sheds.

Trapdoor spiders build burrows with a trapdoor lid over the entrance.

Bird-dung spiders

Bird-dung spiders look like bird droppings. Their **cephalothorax** and **abdomen** are coloured just like a bird dropping, and are a lumpy shape. This protects them from **predators** such as birds, which do not notice them.

Camouflage

Many spiders have shapes, colours and patterns that make them look like they are part of the place where they live. For example, they may be the same colour as the tree trunk they live on. This is called camouflage.

Camouflage protects spiders from animals that might want to eat them. It can also hide them from their **prey** when they are hunting.

This spider is camouflaged on a flower.

Spider body parts

A spider's body has two parts. The first part is made of the head and chest joined together. It is called the **cephalothorax** (sef-a-lo-<u>thor</u>-ax). The second part is called the **abdomen** (<u>ab</u>-da-men).

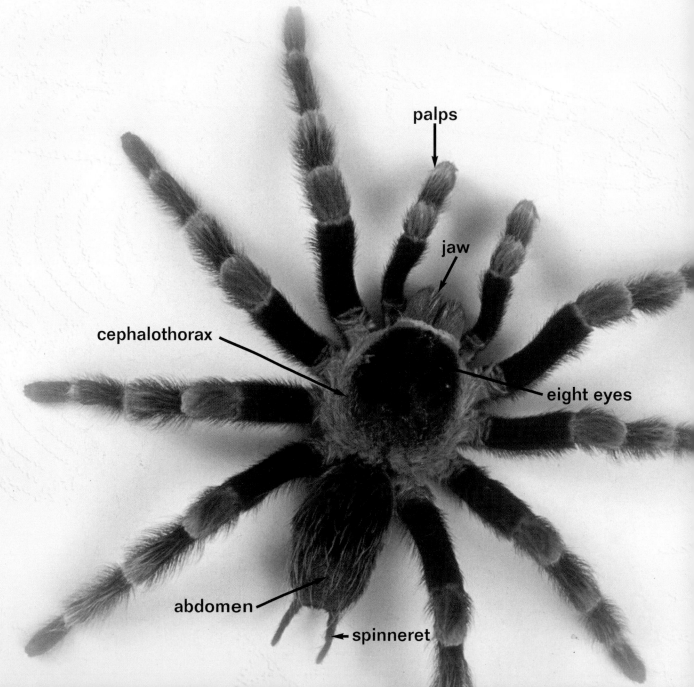

palps

jaw

cephalothorax

eight eyes

abdomen

spinneret

The cephalothorax

A spider's mouthparts and eyes are on the head part of its cephalothorax. Its mouthparts are the mouth, **jaws** and **palps**. There are eight legs joined to the cephalothorax.

The abdomen

On many spiders, the abdomen is larger than the cephalothorax. The abdomen is like a bag and can swell up when it is full of food or eggs. Spiders make silk threads, which come out of special tubes called **spinnerets** at the end of the abdomen.

The exoskeleton

The **exoskeleton** keeps the spider's shape, and stops it from being hurt easily. It also stops the spider from drying out by trapping water inside its body. The exoskeleton is covered with hairs.

Spider mouthparts

A spider has a small mouth underneath its head. On the front of the head it has two **jaws**. On the end of each jaw is a sharp **fang**. Each fang has a tiny tube in it. **Venom** passes down the tube and through a hole near the end of the fang.

Spitting spiders

Spitting spiders spit glue from their fangs. These small spiders can squirt glue for 10 millimetres. They stick down their prey with the glue before biting it.

Spiders bite **prey** with their fangs.

fangs

Palps

A spider has a **palp**, like a finger, on each side of its jaws. The two palps feel and hold food. In some spiders they are quite large, and look like short legs.

The palps have rows of small teeth on them for mashing prey, near where they join on to the head.

A spider uses its palps to move food to its mouth.

Fangs and eating

Spiders eat juices, usually from inside insects. Some spiders can eat other small animals as well, such as frogs and mice.

Venom

When a spider catches its **prey**, it bites with its **fangs**. **Venom** runs down through the fangs, and goes into the animal. The venom stops the prey from moving. It comes from venom **glands** in the spider's head.

Almost all spiders use venom to catch and kill their prey.

Mashing and sucking

The spider then pours juices out of glands in its upper lip. The juices go into the prey and make it mushy. The spider crushes and mashes up the prey with its **jaws** and **palps**.

When the prey is mashed up and juicy, the spider sucks it up through its mouth. The spider's mouth is very small, so it can only eat juices.

This spider is using its palps and jaws to crush its prey before sucking up the juices.

Eight eyes for seeing

Most spiders have eight eyes. They are usually in two rows on the top of the head. There is a front (or lower) row and a back (or upper) row.

A spider can see details with some of its eyes. With its other eyes a spider sees dark and light, and movements in the distance.

Wolf spiders have good eyesight. They have four smaller eyes in front and four larger eyes arranged in a square shape on top of their head.

How well do spiders see?

Most spiders do not see very well. Spiders that live in dark places, or catch their **prey** in webs, do not need to see well. They rely mostly on touch and smell to know what is happening around them. Some spiders that live in dark caves do not even have eyes.

Net-casting spider

A net-casting spider has two huge eyes, so it can see insects at night. It holds a web net between its front feet. When it sees an insect coming, it swoops on it with its net.

small eye

large eye

Hairs for sensing

Spiders **sense** with their hairs, feet and by feeling **vibrations**.

Sensing with hairs

Spiders have hairs all over their bodies. They can touch, taste and hear things with their hairs. Some of the hairs are very thin, and stand up straight. These hairs pick up very small movements of the air around the spider. Some hairs can taste, by touching.

Tasting hairs are spread all over the spider's body.

Sensing with feet

A spider can smell things with tiny holes on its feet. Its feet can also feel whether the air is damp or dry.

Sensing vibrations

A spider feels movement with tiny slits all over its **exoskeleton.** These help a web-building spider feel vibrations made by an insect caught in its web. When it senses the insect, the spider rushes over and catches it.

This is a highly magnified view of a spider's foot, showing the sensing hairs.

Sensing each other

Spiders **communicate** with each other. They may make vibrations, such as tapping on a leaf, or a web, or water. Some spiders make sounds to communicate by rubbing parts of their bodies together. Spiders often touch and stroke each other. They see and smell each other, too.

Eight legs for moving

Spiders can walk and run. Some spiders can jump. Each of a spider's eight legs has seven sections, including the foot. The legs have hairs and **spines** on them.

Web-building spiders

Spiders that catch their **prey** in webs have three claws on the end of each foot. They use these for holding on to the web and on to their prey.

A spider has eight legs joined to its **cephalothorax**.

Hunting spiders

Spiders that hunt down their prey have two claws on the end of each foot. These claws have tiny teeth on them.

Jumping spiders

Jumping spiders catch their prey by jumping on them. Some can jump more than 50 times the length of their body. They push off with their four back legs.

Hunting spiders can also have lots of hair under their feet. These hairs help hold the spider's feet down if they are walking on a surface that is smooth or damp. They also help the spider to hold its prey.

Spiders have claws on the end of each foot for gripping.

Outside and inside a spider

A hard shell covers the back of a spider's **cephalothorax**. The **abdomen** has soft skin.

The heart

A spider has a long, thin heart running down the middle of its abdomen. The heart pumps blood around the body.

How do spiders get air?

Many spiders have lungs. These take in air for the spider, from an air hole called a **spiracle** (<u>spi</u>-rak-el) underneath. Some spiders have tiny tubes that take air into the body through spiracles.

What happens to food?

A spider's food goes from the **sucking stomach** to the food stomach, for it to **digest**. Waste passes out of the **anus** as droppings.

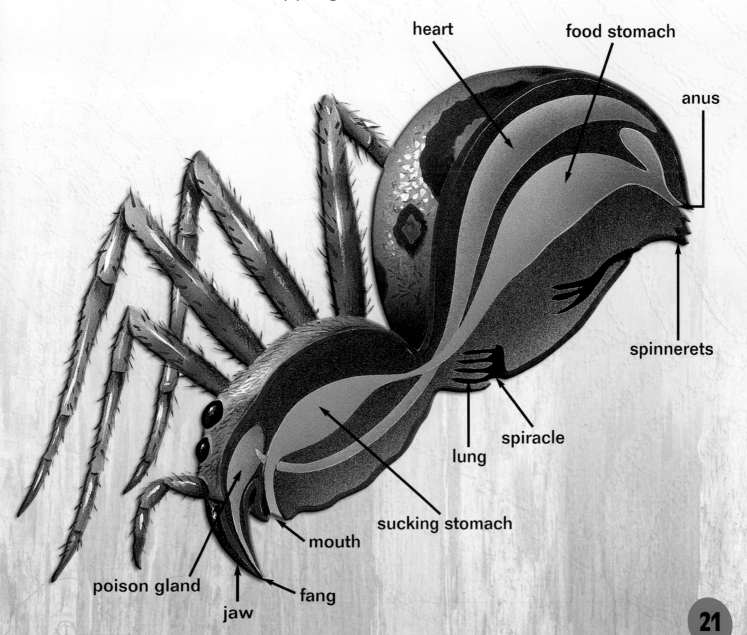

heart

food stomach

anus

spinnerets

spiracle

lung

sucking stomach

mouth

poison gland

jaw

fang

Making silk

All spiders make silk. Spider silk is stronger than steel wire of the same thickness.

A spider makes silk in **glands** in its **abdomen**. Most spiders have three pairs of **spinnerets** at the end of their abdomen. The spinnerets have tiny tubes in them. Different kinds of silk come out of different tubes.

Threads of silk come out of the spinnerets on the abdomen.

What is silk for?

Many spiders build webs with their silk. Spiders also use silk to wrap up their **prey**, to make nests, and to wrap up their eggs. They can also spin out a thread of silk behind them, so they can safely drop down from wherever they are, such as on a leaf or branch.

Ballooning

Some **spiderlings** spin threads of silk and fly in the air with them. This is called ballooning. In summer, the air can be full of spiderlings' silk.

A spider makes different kinds of silk for different uses. Some silk is dry, and some is sticky.

Spinning a web

Different spiders make different kinds of webs to catch food. Webs may be round or fluffy. Others are like sheets. Some spiders make nets, and some make traps.

Orb spiders

Orb spiders make round webs, by building spokes from the centre, like the spokes of a wheel. Then they go around and around the spokes, leaving silk behind them to finish the web. The silk is sticky, to catch insects.

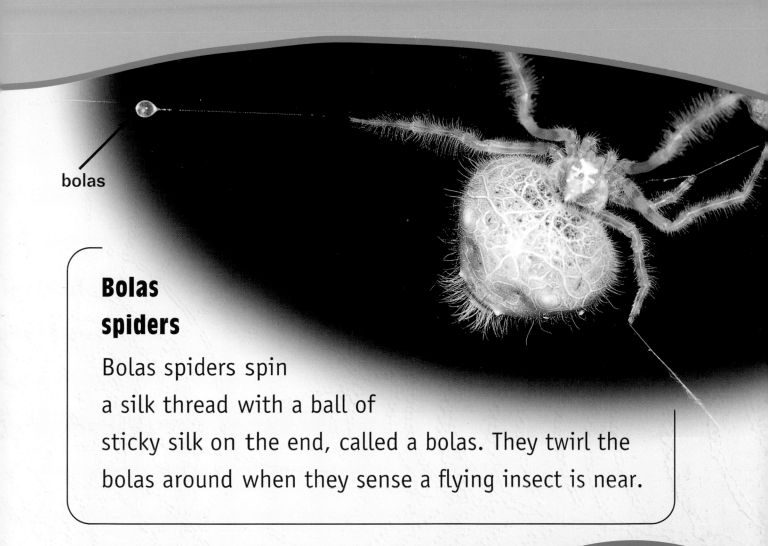

bolas

Bolas spiders

Bolas spiders spin a silk thread with a ball of sticky silk on the end, called a bolas. They twirl the bolas around when they sense a flying insect is near.

Black house spiders

Black house spiders build tangled webs in the corners of windows or inside buildings. The web may have a funnel-shaped section in which the spider shelters. Insects get tangled in these webs.

Life cycle of spiders

Spiders grow from eggs. A female spider **mates** with a male, and then she lays her eggs.

Tiny spiders might lay only one egg. Larger spiders may lay more than 1000 eggs. The female builds a silk egg bag around the eggs and the young spiders start to grow inside. The eggs usually hatch after a few days or weeks. The young spiders are called **spiderlings**.

This egg bag has been opened to show the eggs and spiderlings inside.

Wolf spiders

A female wolf spider carries her egg bag joined to her **spinnerets**. When the eggs hatch, the spiderlings climb on to her back. They ride there for about a week.

Moulting

When the growing spiders are too big for their skin, the skin splits open, and they climb out. This is called moulting. Spiders moult several times as they grow into adults.

This growing spider (below) is shedding its skin (above) for a new and bigger one.

Spiders and us

Many of us are scared of spiders. This may be because of the way they look. It could also be because spiders can move very suddenly.

Can spiders hurt us?

Most spiders will try to run and hide if they are disturbed. Only a few will try to defend themselves.

Most spiders do not bite people. Most of them cannot even break human skin because their **fangs** are too short. A few spiders can kill people, because their **venom** is poisonous to people.

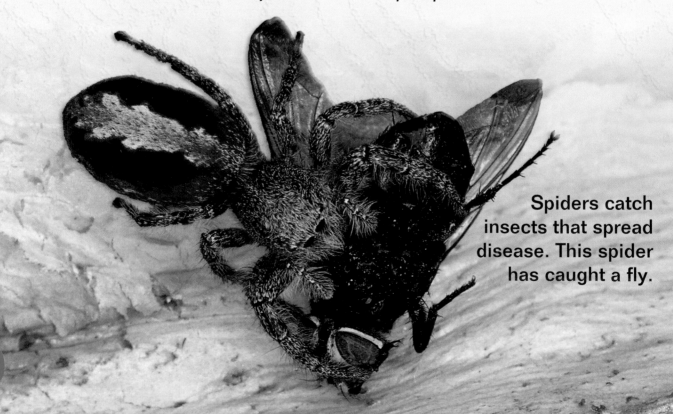

Spiders catch insects that spread disease. This spider has caught a fly.

The next time you see a spider, remember it is probably just looking for something to eat.

Useful spiders

Indoors, spiders catch pests such as flies and mosquitoes. Outdoors, they catch insects that eat garden plants. Spiders are also useful to the animals that eat them!

Find out for yourself

You may be able to find a spider and its web, inside or outdoors. Are there insects caught in the web? Watch the spider and see what it does.

Books to read

Bug Books: Tarantula, Monica Harris (Heinemann Library, 2003)

Looking at Minibeasts: Spiders, Centipedes and Millipedes, Sally Morgan (Belitha Press, 2001)

Using the Internet

Explore the Internet to find more about spiders. Websites can change, so if the links below no longer work, do not worry. Use a search engine, such as www.yahooligans.com or www.internet4kids.com, and type in a keyword such as 'spiders', or the name of a particular spider.

Websites

http://www.enchantedlearning.com/themes/spiders.shtml This site has quizzes, crafts, printouts and other activities to do with the theme of 'spiders'.

http://www.amonline.net.au/spiders This website has lots of information about spiders, photos, fact sheets and useful links.

Glossary

abdomen last of the two main sections of a spider

anus hole in the abdomen through which droppings are passed

cephalothorax spider's body part made of head and chest joined together

communicate send and receive messages

digest break down food so an animal can use it for energy and growth

exoskeleton hard outside skin of a spider

fang pointed tooth

gland part of body that makes something for a special use, such as venom or silk

habitat place where an animal or plant lives

jaw hard mouthpart that moves and has a fang on it

mate when a male and a female come together to produce young

palp small body part like a finger, near a spider's mouth

predator animal that kills and eats another animal

prey animal that is caught and eaten by another animal

sense how an animal knows what is going on around it

species type or kind of animal; animals of the same species can produce young together

spiderling very young spider

spine hard, pointed spike

spinneret body part on the end of a spider's abdomen through which silk passes out

spiracle tiny air hole on a spider's body, which lets air inside

sucking stomach stomach that sucks in a spider's food

venom poison

vibration fast, shaking movement

Index